I feel good ...

100 inspiring actions to bring joy to life

Giek Far Chan

ISBN
ISBN: 978-1-5437-5311-0 (sc)
ISBN: 978-1-5437-5312-7 (hc)
ISBN: 978-1-5437-5310-3 (e)

Print information available on the last page.

To order additional copies of this book, contact
Toll Free 800 101 2657 (Singapore)
Toll Free 1 800 81 7340 (Malaysia)
www.partridgepublishing.com/singapore
orders.singapore@partridgepublishing.com

08/22/2019

PARTRIDGE

I feel good ...

... when I plan ahead.

... when I breathe deeply.

... when I walk around the neighbourhood after a heavy downpour.

... when I have a meal

with someone.

... when I can trust someone.

... when I put in my best effort.

... when I smile and greet.

... when I keep my things organised.

... when I concentrate to accomplish a task.

... when I am at peace
with myself.

... when I design something.

... when I daydream.

... when I am committed.

... when I do what is right.

... when I read the Bible.

... when I obey God.

... when I have a break.

... when I encourage

someone.

... when I am sincere and honest.

... when I help someone.

... when I respect

someone.

... when I manage my time (and my life).

... when I keep my work-

life balance.

... when I am contented and keep a simple life.

... when I am not in debts.

... when I craft something.

... when I read a book.

... when I watch a movie.

... when I colour a picture.

... when I drive around.

... when I take a bus ride.

... when I love someone.

... when I have a haircut.

... when I comb my hair.

... when I look at myself
at the mirror.

... when I wear my
favourites.

GIVE
THANKS

... when I write a
"Thank you" note.

... when I eat healthily.

... when I give.

... when I solve a problem.

... when I creatively do something in a different way.

... when I share what I newly learned.

... when I share my thought.

... when I take ownership.

... when I speak positively.

... when I stroke a cat.

... when I hug someone.

... when I clean my home.

... when I drink water.

... when I have a cup of
hot chocolate.

... when I water the plants.

... when I exercise.

... when I dress up comfortably and appropriately.

... when I write neatly
and read my handwriting.

... when I do a mind map.

... when I see the big picture and the direction.

... when I appreciate the variety of life.

... when I choose
purpose and happiness
at work and in life.

... when I take the initiative.

... when I understand a painful lesson.

... when I have the confidence to move on.

ZzZ

GOOD NIGHT

Zz Z

BIG dream

GOOD NIGHT

Sweet DREAMS

... when I have an early rest at night.

... when I drink a cup of
warm milk.

... when I cook a meal.

... when I smell the trees.

... when I sit on a bench

at the park.

... when I feel the warmth of the sunlight.

... when I see a taking off plane.

... when I take a

boat ride.

... when I reflect on the
blessings in life.

... when I walk on the beach.

... when I look at the

flowers.

... when I appreciate others.

... when I look at a beautiful painting.

... when I reflect
and think.

... when I pause to think before answering.

SEE the WORLD

... when I take a holiday
to the countryside.

... when I have a glass
of wine.

... when I use my favourite pen to write.

... when I care for my family.

... when I have a refreshing bath.

HAPPINESS — IS FOUND WHEN YOU STOP COMPARING YOURSELF — TO OTHER — PEOPLE

... when I do not compare myself with others.

... when I have a good laugh.

... when I discuss to resolve my concern.

... when I learn

something new.

... when I show others
how to carry on.

anticipation

... when I achieve
a goal.

... when I start immediately and do not procrastinate.

... when I do a
DIY project.

... when I use decorative tape.

... when I play ukulele
for the first time.

... when I sing.

... when I look at
the birds.

... when I care by sharing.

... when I speak up
for what is right.

... when I am happy

for other's success.

... when I spend time with like-minded people.

... when I find out on the truth and meaning of life.

... when I am more patient with myself and others.

... when I try.

I feel good when I ....

....

....

....

....

....

....

....

....

That's it, and that's it. You may say "I need to feel good now", "I need to feel better tomorrow", and "I need to feel the best all the time." Is that possible?

Yes, it is, if we conscientiously focus on positive thoughts and take positive actions. You are the one who knows yourself the best as you reflect and get to know your inner self.

This is by no means exhaustive, and you can add more to this list. At one moment, you can also take a few actions that make you feel good at your unique circumstance. What you decide to do, how you do it and when you do it greatly depend on your unique self too. Let's build the habits that lead to an enjoyable life... better thought leads to better action, and a more joyful living.

CPSIA information can be obtained
at www.ICGtesting.com
Printed in the USA
BVHW020000040919
557357BV00019B/273/P